TREASURY OF
Historic Folk Ornament

in Full Color

EDITED BY

Helmuth Theodor Bossert

DOVER PUBLICATIONS, INC.
New York

Published in Canada by General Publishing Company, Ltd., 30 Lesmill Road, Don Mills, Toronto, Ontario.
Published in the United Kingdom by Constable and Company, Ltd., 3 The Lanchesters, 162–164 Fulham Palace Road, London W6 9ER.

Bibliographical Note

This Dover edition, first published in 1996, is a selection of plates from *Das Ornamentwerk*, as described in the Publisher's Note, which was written specially for the Dover edition.

DOVER *Pictorial Archive* SERIES

Library of Congress Cataloging-in-Publication Data

Treasury of historic folk ornament in full color / edited by Helmuth Theodor Bossert.
      p.   cm. — (Dover pictorial archive series)
   "The plates reproduced in this work originally appeared in Das ornamentwerk . . . by Helmuth Theodor Bossert (1889–1961), published in Berlin by E. Wasmuth in 1924"—Pref.
   ISBN 0-486-29094-8 (pbk.)
   1. Decoration and ornament.   I. Bossert, Helmuth Theodor, 1889–1961.
II. Bossert, Helmuth Theodor, 1889–1961.   Ornamentwerk.   III. Series.
NK1530.T74   1996
745.4—dc20   96-4257
                                                       CIP

Manufactured in the United States of America
Dover Publications, Inc., 31 East 2nd Street, Mineola, N.Y. 11501

PUBLISHER'S NOTE

Folk art is the art of the people, as opposed to the highly sophisticated art of a ruling elite or intelligentsia. Long ignored by scholars, its diverse beauties began to gain a wide appreciation in the nineteenth century, in part because of the spread of nationalistic movements throughout Europe. Later, attention was directed toward non-European societies, including those of Africa and Oceania, although a distinction is frequently drawn between folk art and the art of preliterate societies.

There are some characteristics that help to define the nature of folk art. It is generally applied to utilitarian articles—furniture, tools, clothing. Motifs tend to incorporate floral and animal themes. Materials used are those available locally that are most workable. Tradition plays a major role; the artist is not an innovator. Special attention is devoted to items used for ceremonies or festivals, religious art forming a distinct category.

The plates reproduced in this work originally appeared in *Das Ornamentwerk: eine Sammlung angewandter farbiger Ornamente und Dekorationen,* by Helmuth Theodor Bossert (1889–1961), published in Berlin by E. Wasmuth in 1924. That edition contained 120 plates from which the 60 reproduced here have been selected. They are presented in the sequence of the original, which also provided the basis of the captions.

1. Crete and Greece, middle and late Minoan period, ca. 2000 B.C.

2. Greece, Geometric period, 900–700 B.C.

3. Middle East, Hittites.

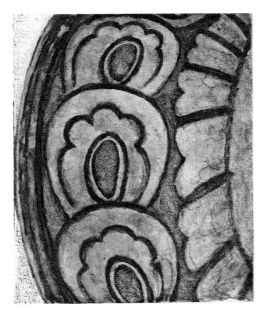

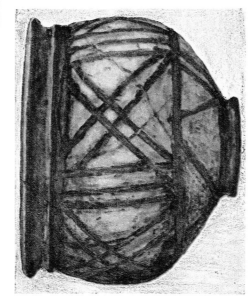

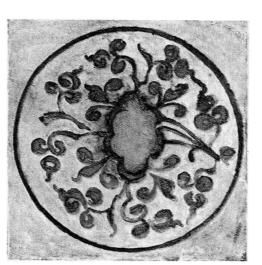

4. Middle East, antiquity and Islamic period.

5. Persia, sixth–eleventh centuries.

6. Egypt, Eighteenth and Nineteenth Dynasties.

7. Egypt, late New Kingdom.

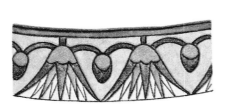
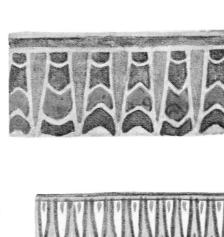
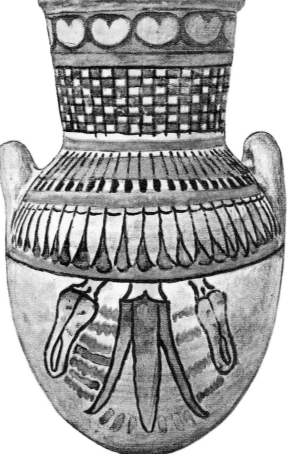

8. Egypt, late New Kingdom.

9. Egypt, Coptic period, third–seventh centuries.

10. Persia, fifteenth–seventeenth centuries.

11. Turkey and Persia, fifteenth–seventeenth centuries.

12. Middle East, Islamic period, thirteenth–sixteenth centuries.

13. Syria (Aleppo), ca. 1600.

14. Northwest Africa, early twentieth century.

15. Africa, Saharan Tuareg and Liberia, early twentieth century.

16. Africa, Niger district, early twentieth century.

17. Africa, Sudan, Congo and Cameroon, early twentieth century.

18. Lithuania (Memel), early twentieth century.

19. Estonian and Finnish, early twentieth century.

20. Russia, early twentieth century.

21. Ukraine, early twentieth century.

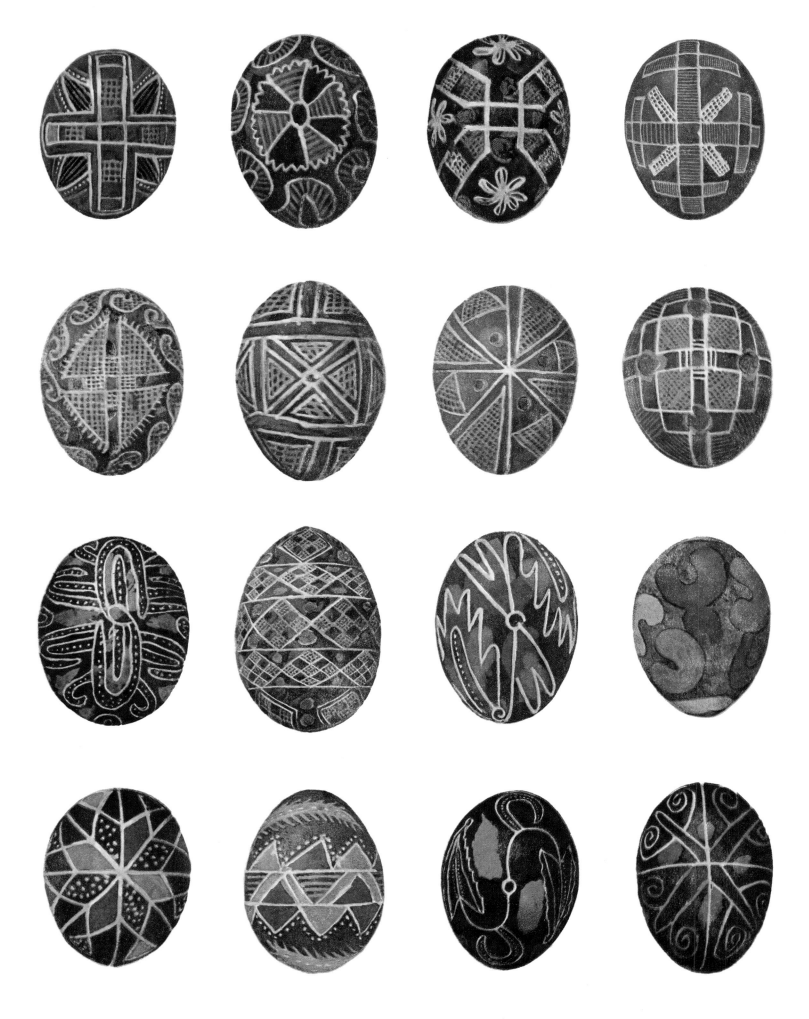

22. Romania (Bukovina), early twentieth century.

23. Dalmatia and Macedonia, early twentieth century.

24. Turkey, Tatariya and Persia, early twentieth century.

25. Lapp and Siberian peoples, early twentieth century.

26. Siberian peoples, early twentieth century.

27. Kirgiz, early twentieth century.

28. Pamir Mountains, early twentieth century.

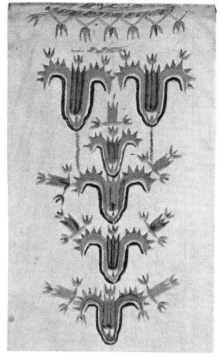
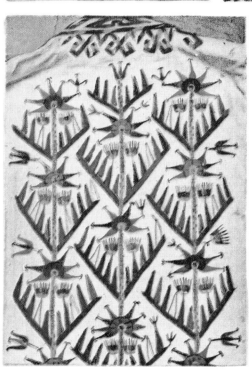

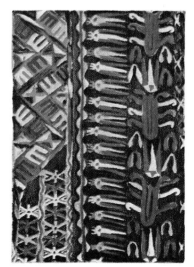

29. Turkmen, early twentieth century.

30. Turkmen and Bukhara, early twentieth century.

31. Bukhara and Samarkand, early twentieth century.

32. Bukhara, early twentieth century.

33. Bukhara, early twentieth century.

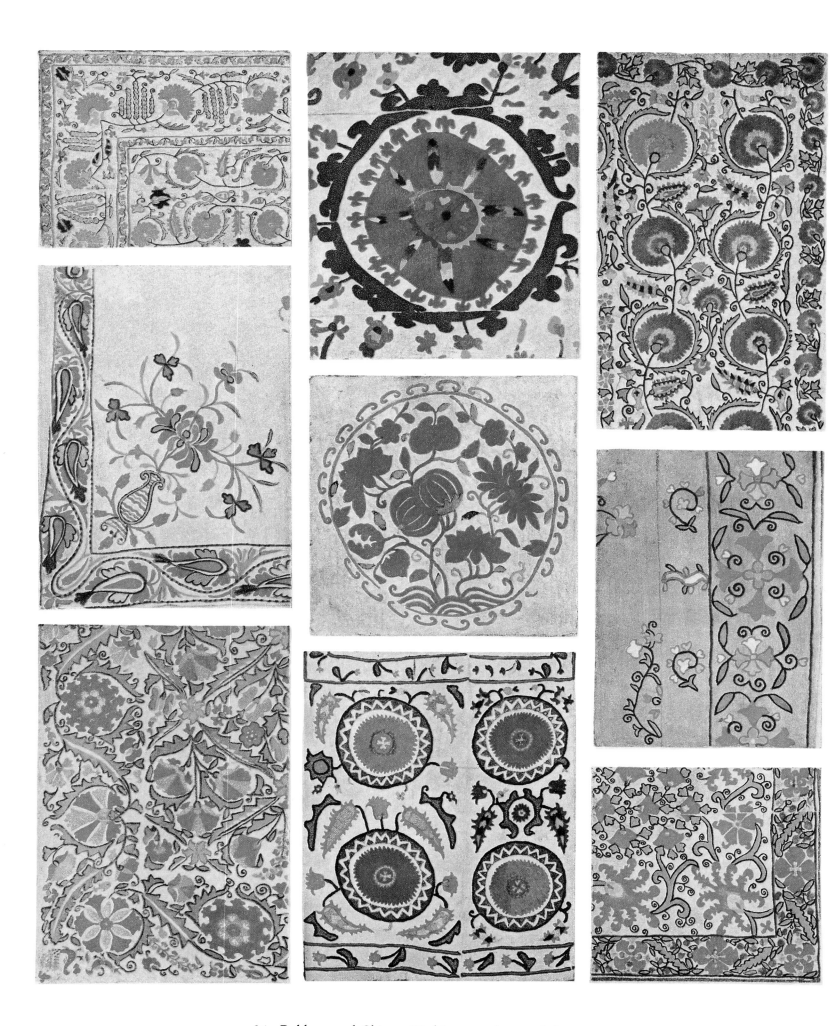

34. Bukhara and Chinese Turkistan, early twentieth century.

35. Chinese Turkistan, early twentieth century.

36. Chinese Turkistan, early twentieth century.

37. Chinese Turkistan and Punjab, early twentieth century.

38. Northeastern India (Assam, Himalayas, etc.), early twentieth century.

39. Ceylon (Kandy), early twentieth century.

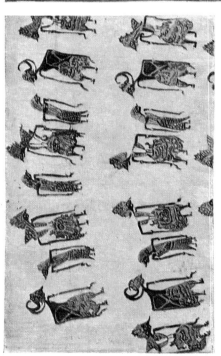

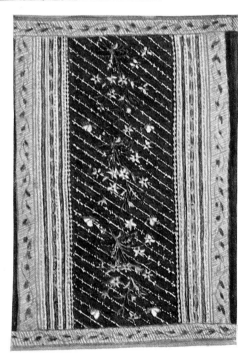

40. Java, early twentieth century.

41. Borneo, early twentieth century.

42. Malay archipelago, early twentieth century.

43. Malay archipelago and Formosa, early twentieth century.

44. Hainan Tao, early twentieth century.

45. Siam, early twentieth century.

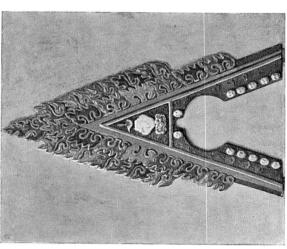

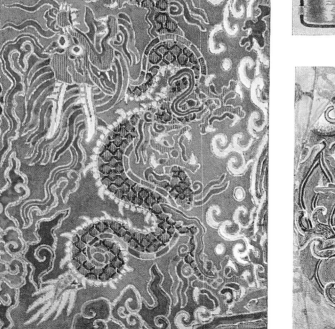

46. Tibet, early twentieth century.

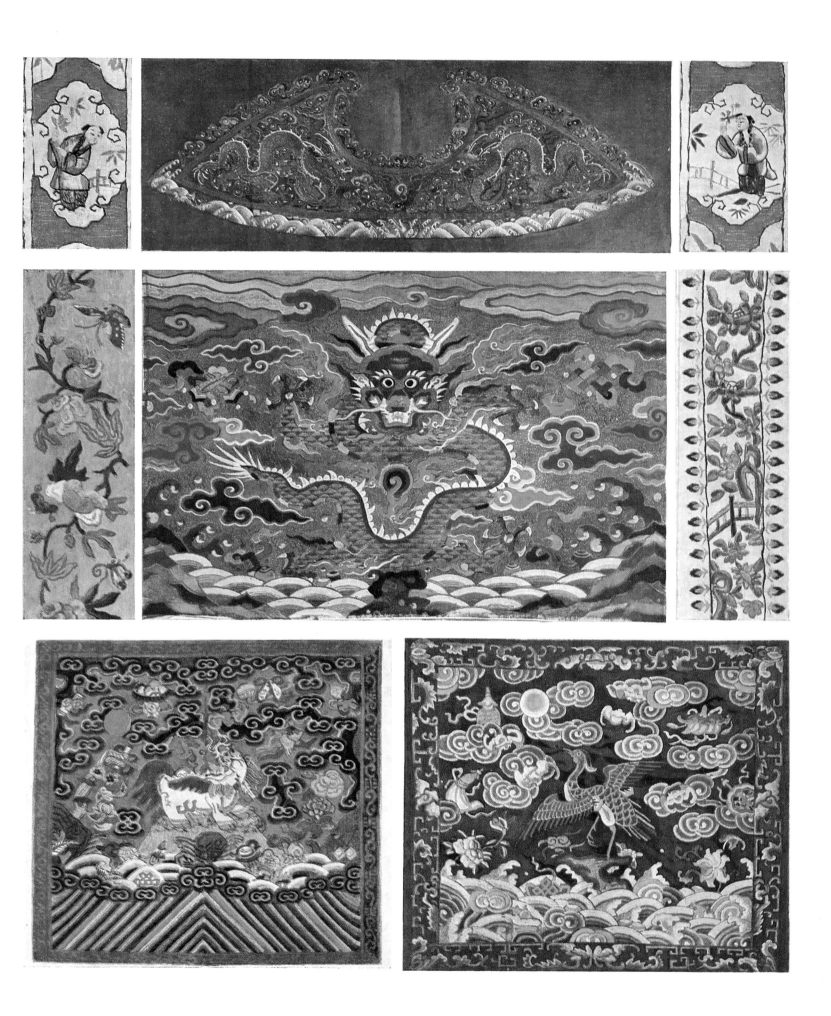

47. China, early twentieth century.

48. China, early twentieth century.

49. Japan, early twentieth century.

50. Japan (Ainu), early twentieth century.

51. Oceania, early twentieth century.

52. Oceania, early twentieth century.

53. New Zealand, nineteenth century.

54. Oceania, early twentieth century.

55. Northwest Pacific coast of America, nineteenth century.

56. Pueblos and California, pre-Columbian and early twentieth century.

57. Mexico and Central America, pre-Columbian.

58. Mexico, Peru, Brazil and Bolivia, pre-Columbian and early twentieth century.

59. Peru (Nazca), pre-Columbian.

60. South America, post-Columbian and modern.